LAUREN BAB

HEY BRIDE...
GET UP AND SPEAK!

Be the Bride who uses their voice to create

a huge impact on their

Wedding Day

Copyright Year: 2021

Copyright Notice: by Lauren Babic. All rights reserved.

The above information forms the copyright notice: © 2021 by Lauren Babic.

All rights reserved.

ISBN 978-6671-1136-0

Photography by Michael Maurer

www.michaelmaurerweddings.com

Instagram: @michaelmaurerweddings

YOU ARE AN ELITE BRIDE

READ THIS BOOK COVER TO COVER SO THAT YOU TOO CAN GET UP AND SPEAK!

Dedication to
The Father of The Bride

My dad, Mark Hobbs is the most positive person I know and I'm so grateful for this attitude which he has instilled in me over the years. He started with very little and worked extremely hard to build a life of wealth and fortune. The more successful he becomes the more he gives away. He has supported many thousands of people, either through Charities or just by helping people where he can. He has created and distributed care packs for the homeless, and he volunteers on his 'blood bike' to race blood to people in desperate need, to hospitals in and around Essex & London. He created a 'church without walls' which was intended to be for people who couldn't get to church in person and needed a way to hear the Word from their homes. This was made available through his online church service which was in fact the first online congregation in the world – much before the Pandemic of Covid-19 in 2020.

Few people realise how much he does for others because he doesn't brag about helping them in order to get praise as it is a natural part of his day. I believe he is where he is in life not only because of his positive mindset and hardworking nature, but mainly because he truly cares about people. So, I want to dedicate this book to him, to put a **HUGE** spotlight on my amazing dad, **NOT ONLY** to thank him for being the ultimate example of what a father should be to his daughter but also to say **SORRY** for stealing the limelight on one of the most important days of his life - his daughter's wedding day!

I'm sorry Dad, but my speech outshone yours, and so I thought it would only be fair to give you a boost here. As I know you waited years to do **YOUR** speech of a lifetime; it's just funny that I chose to do **MINE** on the same day - like father like daughter I suppose - **I LOVE YOU DAD!**

I PRAY ALL BRIDES GET TO EXPERIENCE THE JOY OF HAVING A FATHER LIKE MINE

Hey you!

Let me first of all tell you, the fact you chose to pick up this book shows you're not just any bride. You my dear, are a **UNIQUE** bride in this world. You're on the right track to adding something fresh, exciting, memorable and downright empowering to your perfect day…Yes, that's right **YOUR** Wedding Day.

You have organised everything down to a 'T'. Finally, you can sign off your wedding admin as complete. You're ready and you know it's going to be an incredible day. Here's the thing… I think there is one jewel of entertainment you haven't thought of yet, which you could add, to get your day to the top of the wedding memory leader board and guess what…it's **FREE!!**

Do you want to surprise your family and guests with something that isn't at all traditional, but something that could, at the end of the day, be the absolute highlight **OF** the day because it was so unexpected?

Do you want to know what's missing from your wedding, to give it the ultimate high vibe bride experience that your guests will never forget?

Bride it's your day to shine. It's time for your Wedding Speech! Yes, that's right, I want you to get up and speak your bridal truth!

Lauren x

RISE UP!

BRIDE YOU BETTER RISE from your seat and speak to the people who you love most dearly! Bride, how can you do this by sitting there at the table quietly listening to everyone else thanking *YOUR GUESTS AND BRIDESMAIDS* for showing up? Not to mention, it's just another perfect moment in the day for everyone to see how utterly stunning your dress is. It would otherwise be creased from all that time you would have been seated.

Your Wedding Day is one of the **BEST** days in your life! It is truly magical finding a partner in this world that you absolutely cannot begin another day of your life without. Don't you want to declare your undeniably deep affection for your partner, and how grateful you are that you are now a married couple about to take on the world together? There's nothing better than telling them how intensely in love you are with them, it just makes it that little bit extra special on your wedding day, witnessed by all your favourite friends and family. If the person you're marrying makes your day better by just being part of it, this is your moment to make sure they know it.

I want you to join me in the role of the bride who spoke without fear and in turn made every one of her guests howl with laughter. Let your guests hear real love pour from your mouth into the ears of the people you adore. My dad has even admitted to me he thinks my speech trumped his, but he has forgiven me for stealing the limelight and has confessed how much he absolutely loved it.

In this book I have written out my own bride's speech just for you; to inspire you and show you that you can do it too! Let it help you reach a new potential you never knew you had. I didn't realise I could make people laugh so much and it really was a delight for me. I would never have known this about myself if I hadn't read my speech out loud! I really hope you enjoy reading my speech and I encourage you to step out of your comfort zone and write your own.

Another reason I created this book was to be super real with my brides-to-be and to let you know, things often don't quite go according to plan at weddings…but don't worry because that one hiccup might just make your whole wedding. Hiccups lead to the best stories and make for an **AWESOME** speech - I'm telling you this from experience, if you keep reading, you'll see.

Listen…you're the one who has put in so much effort for the wedding of your dreams, now add some fireworks and stand up. Get ready to write the speech of a lifetime. **GRAB THAT MIC.** It's your turn to talk.

Hear me cheer for you as your inner voice shouting

"HEY BRIDE… GET UP AND SPEAK!"

YOUR FA
GU
FOR
NOT SO
BR

IL - SAFE
IDE
THE
MUTE
IDE

"BRIDE, CAN YOU KEEP A SECRET?"

Speeches can be a lot of pressure, a bit stuffy and actually downright stressful to write at times. This is where I come in, to help you realise you can do it. You just need to take a breath, write down what you would say (in your own words) rather than what you *think* you should say and definitely don't overthink it – just start.

1. THE BRIDE'S SECRET

Bride, I'm about to reveal my top tip and you don't even need to pick up a pen to write anything down yet! So, before you start writing your speech, I need to disclose some super important information to you and if you choose to accept it, the impact it will have on your wedding day will be priceless. You're going to have to trust me! My advice for this whole bridal speech you are about to write is; to keep it a **SECRET FROM EVERYONE**. Don't tell a soul that you will be doing a speech (except the host who will be organising your intro or mic placement etc. See step 3.) The surprise on your guests' faces will make this so worthwhile and I swear you'll enjoy the experience a lot more! By keeping this from everyone, it means you can also back out if you feel too nervous…**BUT DON'T**, stay strong. I believe every beautiful bride can deliver.

2. CREATE YOUR BRIDAL SPACE

My second tip is to go into this with a positive mindset. You can do this! Use the tips from this Fail-Safe Guide, **BELIEVE IN YOURSELF** and the words will flow from your heart. What you hope to say will come easier to you if you are happy and relaxed with a **POSITIVE ATTITUDE**. Treat yourself to a notebook of dreams (mine was pink and sparkly), and a pen that will be used especially for writing your speech. Clear your workspace, light a favourite scented candle and put on some music. Take three breaths in and three breaths out and put your pen to paper. You can do this!

3. GET READY TO RISE

Okay my bride-to-be, you have enough to deal with on your big day so don't be stressed with your speech, or worrying about when you are going to rise up and start speaking. Firstly, make sure you know clearly in your mind at which point during the speeches you want to deliver yours; at the start, in the middle or at the very end. Communicate with the MC (Master of Ceremonies) of your wedding or someone who is in charge of hosting your reception and ask them to introduce you and offer a microphone to you at the decided time. I chose to stand up right at the end of all the speeches after the 'Best Man's Speech' just for the extra surprise factor. When it comes to **THE DAY,** use love as your driving force to raise you up from your seat.

"IT'S YOUR TURN TO TALK"

4. MAKE YOURSELF KNOWN AND YOUR VOICE HEARD

Well, your intro starts with you rising from your seat. You will already have everyone's attention and you haven't even opened your mouth yet! You will have stolen the show already – all you will have to do is start speaking. The thing is, you're probably thinking it's going to be the scariest public speaking, nerve wracking sort of situation you'll ever have to do, but let me tell you it's nothing of the sort. Every single person sitting in front of you loves you and has accepted your invitation to dress up and travel to your wedding, whether that be near or far. They want to be there to support you. If your friends are judgy, well, I suggest you delete them from your life to be honest…*ain't no bride got time for that*. You will realise as soon as you stand up, your guests will be totally excited for you, especially as it is so unexpected for the bride to stand up and produce a speech.

They will be listening with ears wide open full of excitement for you! After you have enjoyed the response you get just from rising for your speech of a lifetime, you can thank your bridesmaids for everything you might have put them through if you were a "Bridezilla", or if you gave them jobs to accomplish throughout the wedding. **THOSE ABSOLUTE GEMS HAVE WORKED HARD FOR YOU BRIDE, THANK THEM, OKAY.**

With a huge smile on your face, thank everyone that **YOU** want to thank and don't let others do it on your behalf. It will also be seriously refreshing to get a woman's perspective on the day as usually speeches are predominantly from a male's perspective. It doesn't matter how many times your bridesmaids are thanked. The whole point is, the appreciation is genuine and heartfelt and coming from **YOU,** the person who knows them better than anyone else on the top table doing a speech.

5. THE IN-LAWS

Now, the in-laws for some might be hard to thank, as they are not always your cup of tea. **LET'S BE REAL**, if you are a bride who doesn't particularly get on well with your in-laws, just blooming thank them and be **GRATEFUL** they have brought up this incredible human being who you are going to spend the rest of your life with. These in-laws of yours are amazing for creating a masterpiece, perfect for you. **JUST LET THAT SINK IN** for a moment and this part of your speech might come easier to you.

If you love your in-laws, by all means, shout to the high heavens about how much you love them; writing this part will be easy for you. If there is a brother, sister or cousin of your partner who you particularly like, go all out in mentioning them here. Thank them for welcoming you into their family so warmly, and tell them how excited you are to have them as your new extended family. At this point of your speech, you can make a remark on your new surname if it has an intriguing meaning to it - you can share this with your guests to tell them something new and interesting. After all, it's your name now too.

"THANK THEM AND BE GRATEFUL"

6. YOUR SOULMATE

Here comes the lovey-dovey part when writing your speech. This section is all about your newly married team mate in life. Now, think about it, they will be giving a beautiful speech about how much they love you, witnessed by all your family and friends; don't you think it's only fair you do the same for them? **YES!**

So, when writing this part of your speech, I want you to think about all the qualities your partner has, that led you to the moment you said **YES**. They have proved themselves to you and you have put your **TRUST** in them. The one and only person in the whole world you want to spend the rest of your life with.

Thank them for finding you and loving you and **MEAN IT.** The intention of your words for this part of your speech are to make your partner feel abundantly loved because they deserve it!

7. FIND HUMOUR IN THE WEDDING DAY HICCUPS

Okay, I am not telling you to look up a load of cringey cliché jokes and just randomly slide them into your speech. At this point, I want you to speak off the cuff. To prepare for this section just write a bullet point attached to the sentence - **'What happened that made me laugh today?'** This could be an opportunity for you to have a laugh with your guests.

This will also help you to be a bride present in the moment taking in all the parts of your day. It could be something that happens in the morning, getting ready with your bridal party or something that might happen in your service or reception before finding your seats to eat.

I want you to stay positive. If something doesn't quite go to plan on your wedding day, don't worry! You can use this as ammunition for a great part of your speech. Trust me, everyone loves a bride who owns their day and can accept, that as much as they strive for perfection, some things are out of their control and actually make for outrageously hilarious moments. (Once you've collected your thoughts, calmed yourself down and can see the funny side of course haha.)

Bride, don't get stressed out by this section. If on the day, you find yourself staring down at your notebook, re-reading the bullet point, remember you have the choice to quickly turn the page and no-one will know you skipped anything! Being funny is great, but it's not the be all and end all of your bridal speech. Being **THANKFUL** and **GRATEFUL** is the heart of your speech - this is more important than having something funny to say.

8. HEARTFELT THANK YOU'S

Thank the people who have helped make your big day become a reality, in my case I thanked my mum and dad. Declare your love for them and thank them for everything they have done for you and how they have contributed to your life. Thank them for accepting your soulmate into their lives, as the perfect choice of a life partner for the beautiful bride standing before them. Make it **MEANINGFUL** and **GENUINE** and you won't go wrong.

9. THE PEOPLE WHO MADE THE CUT

You have done so well you're all the way to tip number 9. If you have followed this guide in chronological order just look at how much you have written out already! Congratulations for committing yourself to this!

Here you can express your sincere gratitude and thankfulness to the ladies and gentlemen, who have accepted your invitation to honour your bridal status, by showing up and supporting you on this important day. It is especially important, to thank those who are flying across countries or continents to make it to your wedding day. Make sure you note those extremely important people down because they are the special ones you need to make more time for. These friends in particular need to know how much you appreciate them, so do keep this in mind when writing your speech. The friends you have invited to your wedding have officially made the cut to live out your **WEDDING DAY DREAMS** with you. These fine friends have made such an impact on your life, that you wouldn't dream of having them miss sharing in such a pivotal moment with you.

10. BEFORE YOU TAKE YOUR BRIDAL BOW

To help close your speech, be inspired by love. The thoughts of love for your friends and family, will spring all the right ideas into permanent ink, on your now not so blank notebook. When you're guided by this love you won't believe how much you have to write!

You can put a spotlight on the people in your life who have demonstrated the type of love you have always aspired to achieve. This could be your parents, grandparents, family friends, or a favourite couple out of your friends who have been an example to you.

When writing about them in your speech, think about how their love has created such a high value point for your marriage and has led you on your path to find your perfect partner for whom you will always be grateful. This will empower you to create a fulfilling, genuine and beautiful end to your bridal speech.

11. INSPIRE & SPARKLE

Now that you have used this guide to help motivate you to write out your speech section by section, I'm happy to say you're almost finished! Bride, you yourself will be an inspiration from the moment you make the decision to stand and boldly start speaking in front of your guests! It is quite possible that you will have guests seated in front of you who are not yet married, and so without even realising it, you may inspire them to also write a bridal speech of their own. They will leave your wedding feeling totally uplifted and filled with confidence, that they too could do what you did and be excited to take on the challenge themselves! *If that's the case, drop them a hint about this book, will you?*

The final thing I want you to remember when you're speaking, is to smile and use eye contact with your guests around the room or area you're using. Genuinely be yourself, but most of all, no matter what, enjoy every minute of delivering your party trick which of course is this secret speech. I'm so excited for you! You are going to **SHINE MY BRIDE**.

READY?

Okay Brides, I hope you now see a wonderful speech written down before you in your notebook! You did it! You're half way there. Now all you have to do is get up and speak! On the day, you will find the magic within you, to carry you through your speech to become an elite bride, who sparkles brighter than the rest. Bride you matter! People definitely want to hear your voice especially on your wedding day so now is the time to break with tradition and choose **NOT** to be a mute bride!

On the next page is my example for you. It's my speech from my wedding day. Read it, enjoy it, look at the pictures to bring it to life and hopefully, it will help you to find **YOUR** voice and to stand up as a **BRIDE FULL OF PURPOSE,** knowing that you alone are capable of bringing magic into the room.

"MRS BABIC THE BAD BITCH"

"Hello Babies...

Ok...I want to start off my marriage by saying more than *'I Will'*". (*Dusko, my husband now stands up beside me for some reason.*) "Babe you don't have to stand up this is my speech now." (*I whisper to him gently*) "Babe I was just making eye contact with you to let you know that I wanted to say more than *'I Will'* today so that's why I turned to look at you, you can sit down now bubba." (*Dusko proceeds to sit back down whilst blushing.*)

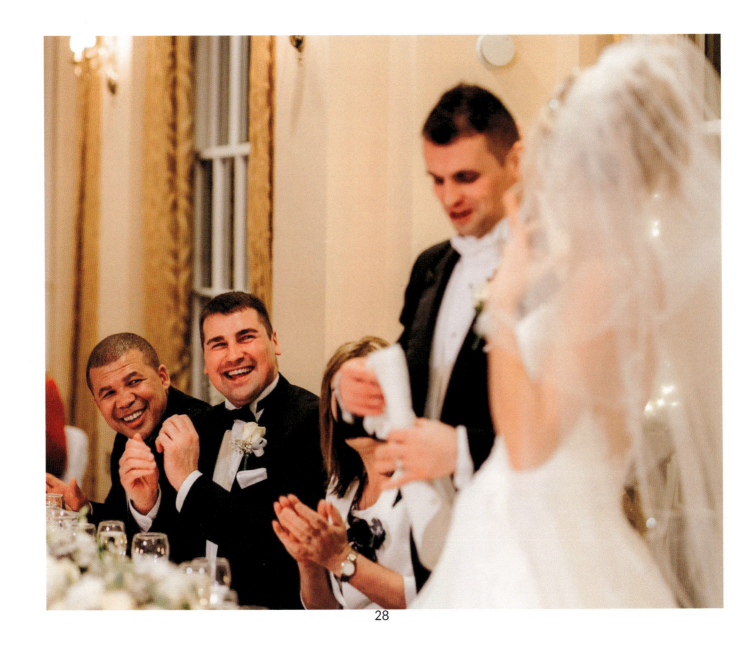

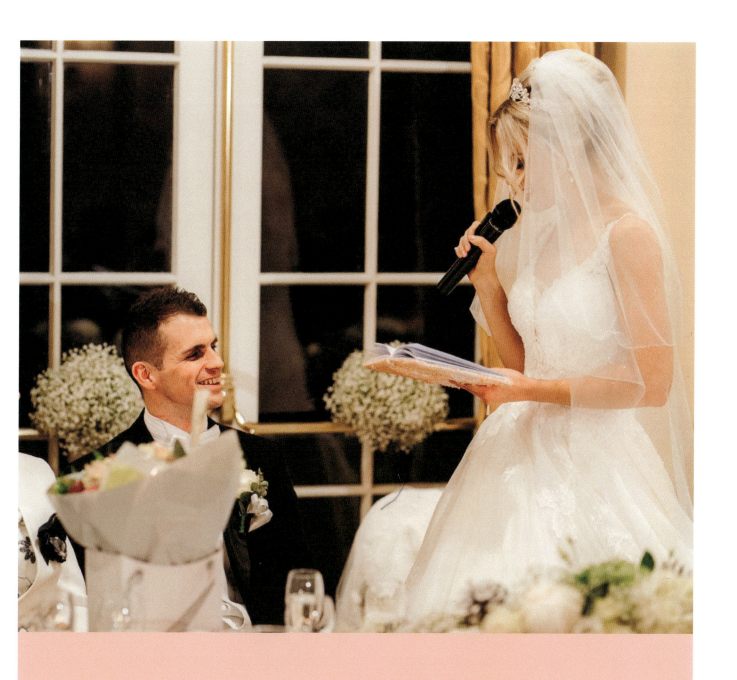

"THIS IS MY SPEECH NOW!"

LAUGHTER ERUPTS IN THE ROOM

"Uh-Hum" (*I clear my throat*) "I digress...all I've said today is *'I Will'* and listen to everyone else thanking all my friends for coming and do you know what... **I wanna** say something as well. Why can't the bride say something at her own wedding? These guys sitting on this top table with me have no clue what's happening here. It was all a secret!" *Dusko looks up to me and says* "I'm a little bit worried about this to be honest!" (*At this point my good friend Eleanor Bechthold shouts out "hashtag strongwoman!"*)

"Thank you, Eleanor, I don't know if it's going to be any good but here goes...

So firstly, obviously I want to thank you all for coming because you're all *my* blooming friends. I know, obviously you're here for Dusko as well, but you're my friends too and *I* haven't thanked you yet. Okay, so that's that, thank you guys; honestly, it means such a lot...**SUCH A LOT I LOVE YOU ALL** - that's why you're here. You are the crème de la crème of friendships so you made the cut! Well done! Otherwise you wouldn't be here... because I wouldn't have invited you..."

LOUD LAUGHTER FROM MY GUESTS AND ME LAUGHING TO MYSELF DOWN THE MICROPHONE

"Okay, so this is what I've written here in my little notebook…right…You're our favourite people in the whole wide world, so it means so much to have you here to support this marriage and all be sitting here in one…orangery." *(I gesture with arms wide to the room that we are all in.)* "I want to thank…*(I pause)* now I know these girls have already been thanked but *I wanna* do it, so, thank you to my Princess Bridesmaids. I adore you all and love you all so much. You look so beautiful…**SOOO** beautiful and you've really rocked it today! You had to take your dresses away and make them fit you because they were all a little too big or a little too long, so, thank you, you've really worked hard to make them look amazing. You've all looked after me and made sure I'm okay throughout the day so, I'm truly grateful. I just want to say a special thanks to my Maid of Honour Natasha over there *(I nod in her direction)* and my Chief Bridesmaid Grace Hatley over there *(I point in her direction)*. I really appreciate both of you and all my other 6 bridesmaids as well, obviously. So just to clarify I sincerely appreciate you all and I'm very grateful for all of you in my life."

"I would like to say a huge thank you to my new Mother-in-law Neda and the Babic family for welcoming me into their home with open arms. I love you all and I'm so happy to now call you my family. One more thing, how beautiful do the girls in the Babic family look…**Oh, My Goodness Me!**" *(Dusko shouts up at me)* "You're a Babic now!" "**OOOHHH** yes babe" *(I squeal)* "**I AM A BABIC NOW** and do you know what Babic means in the Urban Dictionary? I only know this because my brother told me! So, he told me…well it's a bit naughty but it means…. right just a quick warning what with the kiddies around…I'm about to swear…it means **BAD BITCH** actually."

THE GUESTS LAUGH OUT LOUD

"Yeah, in the 'Urban Dictionary' it says something like that. So, apparently, it means like…don't stand in her way because she might set you on fire if you annoy her and stuff. So, I quite like it. In the first instance, I was a bit like, oh, I'm not sure about that. I'm too much of a princess for that sort of name, but do you know what Chelsea Coyne *(I nod and lock eyes with my beautiful friend Chelsea, sitting at the table opposite me)*, I quite like it now baby."

AGAIN, LAUGHTER FILLS THE ROOM

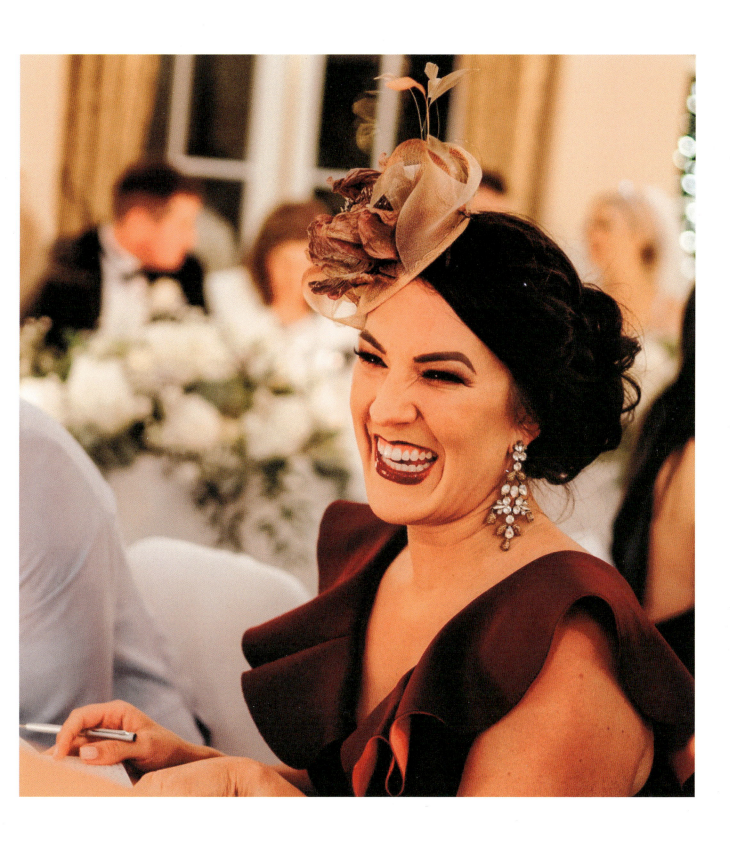

"So next...

oh yes, now, I wrote a little letter to my husband... *(I pause and refocus)*. To my new husband, and oh look, it's here *(a piece of tatty lined paper falls out of my notebook at this point)*, it's fallen out of my book... wait a sec." *(I turn to Dusko)* "Dusko, you can keep this paper I wrote on if you want to, for a keepsake?" *(I turn to him and give him the scrap paper draft of my speech, before I officially wrote it down in my notebook)*. "Yes, this is about **YOU** bubba, *(facing him feeling all giddy and excited)* you're **MY HUSBAND!** It's so cool!"

"Okay here goes..." *(at this point I'm just flicking through my notebook to find where I'm at as I lost the page briefly in my excitement.)* "So, in my pink sparkly sequined notebook it says...To my incredible, brand spanking new husband, you chose me to spend the rest of your life with and I'm so, so grateful babe. Thank you for choosing me to be the woman who gets to experience a life with you, by your side, forever and always. You truly complete me baby, and I am so excited for what we can contribute to our world together, as one. I want to thank you for being patient, caring, honest and loyal to me, since the day we first started our relationship, even when we were apart for months on end with work. You really are the love of my life. I never knew I needed this kind of love until I met you. So, thank you from the bottom of my heart, for showing me what real 100% true love is.

I really feel I am the luckiest woman alive no matter how cliché that is. Dusko, I will support you unconditionally with any ventures you want to pursue in life, and I promise to love you beyond eternity babe. I found agreeing to become your wife, the easiest decision I have ever had to make for myself, and I cannot believe how lucky I am that you asked little old me, out of all the women in this world to enjoy it with and I know how well travelled you are!" *(I laugh out loud at that remark.)* "No, but Dusko in all seriousness, I honestly just cannot wait to begin our life together as a married couple. Dusko, baby you are my greatest joy and my prized possession. I truly do believe you are the man God created to be my perfect match on this earth. I love you so much baby…your forever wife, Mrs Babic." ***(Dusko now stands and we share a MASSIVE KISS at this point.)***

"OH LOVE, I JUST SAT DOWN"

"Okay now...so, guys ...this part is for my beautiful Nan. So, she was supposed to be my flower girl today right...so, here's the story; I was in the blooming church at the end yeah, waiting to see her...and then I say to her, "Oh Nan how did the flower girl bit go?" she's like "Oh nah love I just sat down."

MY GUESTS LAUGH OUT LOUD, IT WAS HILARIOUS

And I was like **"NAANN WHAT??** What the heck happened?" Anyway, guys long story short, it didn't go to plan, right... but, in this notebook that I am holding, is what I was *supposed* to say to her, *if* she *had* completed the role of my flower girl. What she was supposed to do, was pick up the basket in the church, that *wasn't there*, with the petals inside, and then she was supposed to walk down the aisle and sprinkle the petals on the floor, leading my bridesmaids down the aisle...so, can we all just **PRETEND** that my Nan did that while I read this out...yeah? This is what I would have said, if she *had* completed her role as my flower girl today. Ready?"

YET AGAIN, THE WHOLE ROOM ERRUPTS WITH LAUGHTER

(I turn to face my Nan) "Hey Nanny... right...To my Nan, thank you for being our flower girl today...

MY GUESTS HOWL WITH LAUGHTER

(I turn to speak to my other guests) I mean I would have loved it if she actually *was* my flower girl and did it in *real* life but we are just ganna pretend today okay? I wouldn't have seen it anyway so I would never have known until I watched my wedding video, but she just came and told me that she didn't do her duties as flower girl, **TO MY FACE**, at the end of the church service like it was nothing!"

MORE LAUGHTER FROM MY GUESTS

"Ok, so back to Nan - Nanny, you are the lead woman in our family, so, I only felt it right to have you lead out my bridal party - *which of course you didn't do*, but **IT'S OKAY BABE** because I didn't know it all went tits up at the time anyway."

LAUGHTER FROM MY GUESTS GETS SUPER LOUD AT THIS POINT

"Nan, I admire you so much, you're strong, graceful and determined. You've been through such a lot and your strength throughout has been inspiring to say the least. I love you and I have been thinking about my lovely Grandad and I know he would have absolutely adored Dusko." *(This is when I started to get emotional.)*

"I LOVE AMERICANS!"

"Oh, I'm all 'emo' now innit… Okay Mummy and Daddy it's your turn."

(I start reading what I see in my notebook, out loud.) "**WOW** I've put in capital letters and two exclamation marks next to it. Mum and Dad, thank you for throwing our dream wedding. Thank you for always making my happiness your highest priority and for the continuous love and support that you have given us as a couple." *(I'm laughing and crying at this point.)* "Oh my goodness, I sound so American!" *(I start laughing out loud along with my guests, **FORGETTING** I have a couple of American guests who have come to our wedding sitting right in front of me.)*

"Nooo guys…I didn't mean anything bad by that! You know when you're watching YouTube, *(I explained)* …and all the American couples at their weddings are crying when they declare their love to each other? I've been watching all the weddings on YouTube and all the couples are from America and they all cry! That's why I said that." *(I'm laughing my head off at this point and looking at my American friends at the table across from me.)* "Erase that guys, **I LOVE AMERICANS!** I don't know why I said that. No, but truly I love Americans; I feel bad now…moving on Chels and Jonathon…delete from your minds, **DELETE.**"

(As I'm laughing under my breath, I can hear my cousin Brad laughing hysterically.) "Brad!!! Stop it!!" *(I shout out at him with a cheeky smile.)*

SO MUCH LAUGHTER FILLS THE ROOM INCLUDING MY AMERICAN FRIENDS

"Okay, Mum's turn; Mummy, you have raised me to be the woman I am today, a lady with class and elegance *(I pause, look around the room and laugh at myself)* but I'm afraid my brothers Dan, Jack and Brad influenced me a bit too much growing up…to be a bit of a ladette - so thanks to all four of you combined for making me turn out to be an attention seeking princess, with a side of **CHAV**."

LAUGHTER FILLS THE ROOM

"Mum you are the most selfless, compassionate, warm hearted woman I have ever met…apart from Anna Walsh over there." *(I point to the table at the back where my incredible friend Anna Walsh is sitting).*

"She's also amazing, but this is my mum we are here to talk about."

AT THIS POINT MY GUESTS ARE OUT OF CONTROL LAUGHING

"This is about my actual mum! So yeah, back to Mum - Mummy, you are the kind of mum who would give up absolutely anything for her children. We all hold mountains of love for you and honestly appreciate everything you do **Every. Single. Day**. Today you have graced us with your radiance and beauty, you are just glowing Mum! Thank you for being my best friend and undeniably adoring mum. I love you so much. I love you more than you could ever imagine, you are amazing and I am so utterly grateful that you are mine."

(I am seriously emotional at this point, trying to hold back tears.) "Daddy Darling… one second, let me pull myself together… Dad, you are one of the most genuine people I have ever known." *(I sniff so loud down the mic as I cry and talk through my wobbly emotional words.)* "I tried to find a man who fit the bill with similar qualities to what you have Dad and I do believe I have finally found these qualities in my Dusko and I am so grateful for this. Dad, I have been so blessed to have you as my dad, a man who has consistently shown his unconditional love for his daughter her whole life. Your unconditional love

for me is the reason I have turned out to be this strong woman you now see standing before you today… right hold on" … *(I pause to take a deep breath)* … "Listen…when Dusko said **'I Will'** today Dad" … *(I pause and get side-tracked for a moment)* "Do you know what, I wanted him to say **'I Do'** but it's **'I Will'**… the Vicar said we cannot use **'I Do'** in the church as it's only for Hollywood movies… so that ended that dream didn't it, never mind."

MY GUESTS LAUGH OUTRAGEOUSLY

"Anyway, when Dusko said…"**I Will**" today Dad, what he was really vowing was to live by the remarkable example you have set. Dusko has tried his best to fill the shoes of someone who he knows is outrageously important to me. I'm talking about you Dad, the man I call my Daddy Darling, the man who has loved me a heck of a lot longer than Dusko! So, he's got a lot of catching up to do! Haha.

What a lot of pressure for Dusko!! Hahaha!! I am so grateful that you both get on so well - like best buds! I couldn't wish for a better husband and a better friendship between both of you. Two extremely important men in my life, I'm beyond grateful that I have you both!"

"Now guys, *(I turn back to address my guests)* … right… it's our wedding today yeah!? Mine and Dusko's big day! But today is actually my mum and dad's anniversary. **YES, IT IS!!** They have been married for 34 years and I hope and pray Dusko and I will love each other as deeply and whole heartedly as they do…". *(I sniff loudly and say down the microphone)* "UUUurrrgghhhh there's bit of bogie coming out, did you see that snot dripping down?!"

MY GUESTS HEARD ME SAY THIS DOWN THE MICROPHONE AND LAUGH LOUDER THAN EVER

My dad says in hysterics "No Lauren, you're doing great, you're doing great just carry on!" *(I start again reading from my notebook)* "Okay, Okay, where was I… after 34 years **FULL STOP**."

LAUGHTER FROM MY GUESTS ERUPT ONCE MORE

"So, Dusko and I have organised something very special for you to commemorate this day. Our amazing, beautiful... give me more adjectives everyone..." *(I ask my guests to shout out only beautiful describing words and I repeat what they offer me)* "stunning, powerful, boss lady, great friend and incredibly talented classical singer is going to sing a song and dedicate it to you. Her name is Chelsea Coyne, she's come all the way from Texas and she kindly said that she would sing for you Mum and Dad to honour this day and your anniversary. So, guys you're really lucky to hear her sing because she's super talented and only gets paid **THE BIG BUCKS!**" *(Chelsea rises from her seat and announces)* "Tina, Mark... Happy Anniversary" *(and closes my speech perfectly, with her beautiful voice).*

YOU HAVE THE POWER TO EXCEED EXPECTATIONS

Thank you, thank you, thank you for reading through to the end of my speech. I truly hope you were able to feel as though you were in the room, there in the moment. I added many photos of my guests so that you could see their genuine reactions and real-life smiles captured throughout my speech. I wanted you, as the reader, to feel as if you were transported directly into the room, to the moment I stood up to reveal the secret I had kept from **EVERYONE,** in order to make the biggest impact possible on my wedding day.

After reading through all the tips from my Fail-Safe Guide, powerful sentences of encouragement and finally my actual speech, I hope you now feel the confidence to get up and speak. Once you've finished reading this pink book, you will have the tools to unleash your unique bridal magnificence, which comes from within you, to create your perfect, authentic, one of a kind bridal speech.

Bride, you've come this far. If you are still doubting yourself and your confidence to do your own epic bridal speech at your wedding, then read on…

You can bring the magic to the room just by being there. You have the power, the courage, the intelligence, the passion and the voice to stand up tall and sprinkle your charm over your adoring guests.

It's your big day so make it count and use your sparkle to leave your guests with a moment they will be talking about for years to come.

Bride, you can make this one, untraditional, powerful change and you absolutely **DO NOT** have to be a particular type of bride to do this! You can be a cocky bride, you can be an attention seeking bride, you can be a feisty bride, you can be a loud bride, you can be a quiet bride, you can be a sassy bride, you can be an emotional bride, you can be a fearless bride - you get the gist.

ALL BRIDES can perform the perfect speech on their wedding day. There is no limit to your magic. I have great faith that you can deliver.

Bride, if you haven't guessed it by now, the magic to your speech is… your personality. That's right, your personality is the one unique gift you have that sets you apart from every other bride in the world. This means the speech you have prepared will be exclusively yours, delivered in your own unique way. Every bride has a personality and every bridal speech will be different and perfect because of their unique magic.

Using my Fail-Safe Guide, **ALL BRIDES** are capable of writing and delivering their own speech at their wedding. So Bride, refer back to this pink book to help you plan out your speech and then use your personality to bring it to life.

Although I cheer for **ALL TYPES** of bride who choose to write a speech for their own Wedding Day, there is one nature of bride in particular who I personally favour to see **ROCK THEIR SPEECH.**

Do you want to know my favourite type of bride to choose to see stand up and speak at their wedding?

It's the painfully shy bride who will read this book from cover to cover, accept the challenge to face their fears, experience personal growth and achieve something life changing, on a day they will never forget.

The guests of this type of bride will glow with happiness to see the person before them shine the light they have been hiding for so long. The impact this bride will have on their wedding day will absolutely blow everyone away. Their guests know they are shy and love this personality trait of theirs, so it would be totally unexpected for them to do a speech at their wedding.

The shock twist would be unforgettable and so powerful. The event will leave guests feeling mountains of love and admiration for their beloved bride standing so confidently before them. It will be an emotional moment for loved ones, who will be captivated by the bride's genuine glow and radiance. The bride will realise it's possible to be shy and shine at the same time. This can be life changing; who knows what this bride will do next.

If you are reading this, and you are my wonderful, vibrant, confident bride, go smash your speech like I know you can. This is a once in a lifetime opportunity so, really enjoy every moment of it. If you are my painfully shy bride reading this, become the highlight of your day and reveal your magic. **YOU,** my beautiful bride, are destined to shine brighter than you ever thought possible. Illuminate the room with your presence, grab your mic and impress your party! Use your personality, big or small to deliver your speech. You're now ready to step into the arena of **ELITE BRIDES** who have had the courage on their wedding day to get up and speak!

YOU CAN

DO IT!

The Editor

Acknowledgements

To my beautiful and talented Sister-in-law and Designer of this book Yvette Hobbs;

A very special thank you for the endless hours sitting next to me editing this book and really honing in on the details I would never have thought of without your skills! I am so grateful for your precious time and efforts making my dreams come true. Your professional accuracy and style has been so inspiring for me. I liken your talent to that of an elite make-up artist accentuating the beautiful bride's features, creating a flawless finish ready for her big day! I'm so thankful for your hard work and dedication and really appreciate everything you have done to create such a special and stylish book for all my wonderful brides-to-be out there. Thank you, thank you, thank you.

To my dad Mark Hobbs, for inspiring me with the idea to release my speech to the world and to just go for it!

To Angela Morrison, for her incredible eye for words and genius suggestions from proof reading my work.

Photography by Michael Maurer

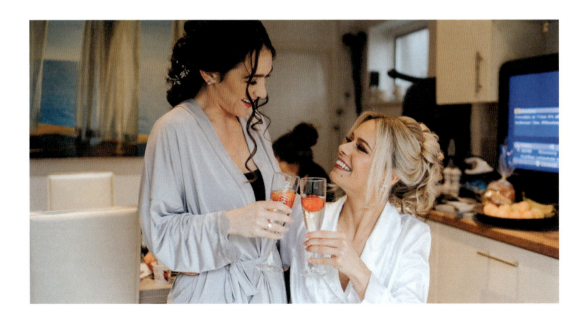

Bride, don't blackout now!

You're about to reveal the **SECRET BRIDAL SNATCH** for your wedding day that will blow everyone away! Now don't ruin the moment by getting drunk and hoping the alcohol will give you the confidence to get you through it. This would be a huge fail. You'll end up slurring your words and destroying what could be a beautiful moment for you and your guests. This is a part of your wedding you want to remember forever. So bride...do it justice. Stay calm. Stay sober.

Let your natural energy get you pumped up for your speech of a lifetime! Listen to your body; you don't need alcohol for the buzz, the rush of adrenaline you will experience will be enough to **BOOST YOUR CONFIDENCE** and accelerate the momentum for you to **GET UP AND SPEAK!**

Feel the goosebumps rising on your arms...that's energy... That's your body's way of saying you're passionate about this speech. You're ready and you want to do this...so don't blackout now.

YOU CAN DO THIS!	YOU CAN DO THIS!
YOU CAN DO THIS!	YOU CAN DO THIS!
YOU CAN DO THIS!	YOU CAN DO THIS!
YOU CAN DO THIS!	YOU CAN DO THIS!

PIECES OF POSITIVITY FOR YOUR BRIDAL BAG

Cut out these small squares of love for an extra boost before you get up and speak!

I am a creative bride and open to change

Today on my Wedding Day, I am fearless

I am loved and respected and my guests want to hear what I have to say

---

I am going to illuminate the room and shine brighter than ever before

---

I am a positive bride and I have so much potential

I am in full control and I know I can do this

I am so excited for this moment to engage with my guests

Printed in Great Britain
by Amazon